# SOUTHERN SENSIBILITY

# SOUTHERN SENSIBILITY

EDITH-ANNE DUNCAN

*photography by* SUSIE PECK AND DUSTIN PECK

Gibbs Smith

First Edition

29 28 27 26 25   6 5 4 3 2

Published by

Gibbs Smith

570 N. Sportsplex Drive

Kaysville, Utah 84037

www.gibbs-smith.com

The authorized representative in the EEA is Simon and Schuster Netherlands BV, Herculesplein 96 3584 AA Utrecht, Netherlands, info@simonandschuster.nl

Designed by Michelle Farinella

Printed and bound in China

This product is made of FSC®-certified and other controlled material.

MIX
Paper | Supporting responsible forestry
FSC
www.fsc.org
FSC® C144853

Library of Congress Control Number: 2024951610

ISBN: 978-1-4236-6795-7

# CONTENTS

# FOREWORD

Don't you love a home that feels inviting, functional, and beautiful as soon as you walk in? It may be bold lacquered paint, graphic wallcoverings, fabulous fabrics, or intriguing art, but the room has a way of welcoming you without being overwhelming, and there is a subtle reveal of detail. In design, there are many constructs to be navigated and balanced to achieve a space that is both innovative and timeless. In her debut book, *Southern Sensibility*, Edith-Anne Duncan provides a comprehensive guide to the details that must be considered to achieve spaces that are remarkable. You'll find nine projects, including second homes, that showcase her deft ability to mix antiques with more modern pieces to create an engaging juxtaposition and tension between different styles.

Duncan's skillful use of color combined with a focus on proportion and scale results in rooms that are elegant, sophisticated, and inviting. What others may consider a problem, Duncan takes on as a challenge to create something distinctive and functional for her client. Her education is steeped in history, and she has the knowledge and experience to know when history bears repeating and when to shake it up. Whether the location is urban, coastal, mountain, or something in between, Duncan delivers a design that is unique and full of personality.

Her love of color and pattern is on generous display in the selections of paint, wallcoverings, fabric, trim, and accessories, which, in a word, make her rooms "joyful." From using a client's favorite color to weave a unifying thread throughout the home to displaying family treasures in a meaningful way, she has a passion for living graciously every day. She excels at fearlessly marrying adventurous colors and patterns in rooms yet still manages to retain the sense of elegance that Southerners are known for.

There is a saying that "rules are made to be broken," but that certainly does not apply to all design decisions. While proportion and scale are the foundation for every room to maintain balance, you can break some rules with dazzling results. Painting a small room a dark color used to be a design "don't," but Duncan proves this approach can also make a small room seem cozy and dramatic.

The level of detail in each space is truly what elevates a good project to a great home. Charles Eames said, "The details are not the details. They make the design." Duncan thrives on the details and offers tips on selecting the perfect light fixtures and lamp-shades, mirrors, hardware, and even the trim on the leading edge of draperies and pillows. She also shares creative problem-solving ideas to design unique spaces to meet individual needs for the homeowners. Duncan worked her magic in her own dining room to create a space that easily transforms to a functional office with a breakfront that offers storage for files and a table that serves as a work surface for meetings. Plus, she creates chic havens for the younger generation as well as for the four-legged family members.

Illustrated examples of inspired design ideas abound in this book and will encourage readers to create spaces that exceed expectations. Duncan's homes are dramatic and comfortable, classic and sophisticated, warm and inviting, and most importantly, a welcoming retreat for the homeowners. She is a master at striking the perfect balance between comfort, beauty, and function.

**Lynn Terry**
Editor, *Southern Home*

Sophisticated, casual interiors with pops of color have always been my design aesthetic. Growing up, my two grandmothers and my father all had a flair for design. While none of them practiced professionally, our family home was always on the local college's annual tour, giving students the opportunity to see an example of a wonderfully decorated interior. It was filled with inherited furnishings mixed with modern touches of chinoiserie. Perhaps the most telling space was the small foyer. Clad in wainscotting with a grass cloth wallcovering, it held a traditional console and mirror that were juxtaposed with an unexpected white leather bench featuring emerald green contrasting piping. This introduction to my childhood home is much like an introduction to my personal style today—many pieces embrace tradition but they are mixed with colorful, charming elements to keep it feeling current and inviting.

Just as my family taught me to appreciate and create beauty, raising my own family has given me the desire and ability to do so with sensibility. Being a mother of twins has taught me a sense of balance between family time, cherished moments, and everyday living. Our pet-friendly home is very approachable but still maintains a level of sophistication. Performance fabrics and wool carpets alongside family heirlooms are a part of everyday living for us. Whether it's an embroidered cocktail napkin or a monogrammed notepad with a beautiful bamboo pen, I feel everyone should live with easy elegance and use the collections and furnishings they have. As my witty mother says, "Use your sterling every day, dear, because if you don't, the second wife will."

Not only is this marriage of beauty and practicality a way of life for my husband, children, and me, it's also the type of home I enjoy creating for my dear clients. Seeing their families thrive and truly live in personalized spaces that have vitality and vibrance gives me great joy—as well as confidence in what I do. I hope you'll find inspiration for your own home among these pages.

**Edith-Anne Duncan**

# 1

# THEN and NOW

MIXING ANTIQUES, VINTAGE, AND MODERN STYLES

Old and new, timeless and modern. I absolutely love the juxtaposition of these elements in a home, and it's a treatment that I use in almost every space I design. When you walk into a room, it's fun to see a few classic elements alongside something a little unexpected or more contemporary like an eye-catching light fixture, a more current finish, or a bold color scheme. I believe it's this mix that gives a space character and personality.

As Southerners, many of us have inherited antique furniture, beloved china patterns, silver services, and even significant art or glassware. We cherish the silver rattles that once belonged to us as children or to our parents and grandparents. We relish dinners around tables that were fixtures in our ancestors' homes. These are things to be celebrated—and they don't have to be put on display but can flow naturally into a design and have everyday use. I often find these pieces are not only functional but have also become a part of us.

While many antiques hold precious places in our memories, we don't want them to feel too precious for use. You should be able to play mahjong on your family game table, relax in your grandmother's favorite armchair, and dine off the plates your parents selected for their wedding china. Why have it if you can't use it?

When I meet a client for the first time, I like to know what heirlooms are important to them, and I immediately begin thinking about how we can reuse or repurpose these in a way that fits their lifestyle. It might be pairing an antique pedestal table with a banquette covered in a durable performance fabric that can stand up to pancakes and sticky syrup with the grandkids or simply placing an acrylic chair next to a nineteenth-century secretary. Whatever the mix is, I want it to feel fresh while keeping the integrity of the piece and being respectful of its heritage at the same time.

These unexpected pairings and applications also make a house feel inviting and personal. There's a sense of approachability that comes from incorporating both new and old. When you reupholster a century-old Chippendale chair or hang an inherited piece of art on a colorful wall, you're bringing it into the here and now. You're saying it's not too delicate or too fine to be used, but rather here to be enjoyed and bring beauty. Isn't that what design is all about?

Reusing and repurposing are at the heart of a Southern home—it's what we do and it's no different when it comes to furnishings. So, don't hide those heirlooms you love in the attic. Bring them out, pair them with colors and fabric you're drawn to, and place them where you can enjoy them every single day.

# ALLEY'S SOUTHERN GRACE

For these dear clients, the phrase "welcome home" was more than just a greeting. With this house, we were actually welcoming the husband back to his home state of Virginia. For more than two decades, the family had lived in South Carolina where they developed a penchant for older, character-rich homes—a category into which their new purchase did not fall. However, it had good bones, and I knew I'd be able to make it fit their style by layering in detailed millwork, timeless patterns, and, of course, those cherished pieces that make a house feel like a home.

My goal here was to use rich wood antiques alongside contemporary finishes and vibrant color to create a look that is playful but also has depth. I immediately saw the opportunity to lean into the bold teal in the dining room, playing it up with a scenic wallpaper and matching high-gloss trim paint that allow the table and chairs to stand out. The bright hue extends across the entry hall into the formal living room where it complements elegant oil portraits of the family.

Throughout the house, older, established pieces are paired with modern lighting and a little bit of sparkle, such as the mirrored wall in the formal living room and the brass cremone bolts in the butler's pantry. After all, if a space was filled with only brown furniture, it could begin to feel like a museum instead of a welcoming home that's full of life.

The clients loved what we did in the original main house so much that we ended up working on an addition after the initial renovation. We created a sunroom that appears to have been here for years, like the house has meandered and been built onto over time. I opted to paint the floors, install a limestone mantel, and build out a coffered ceiling, making it look like we were refreshing the palette, fabrics, and fixtures rather than coming in with a brand-new wing of the house.

This couple loves to host dinners and get-togethers, so that was also an important factor to consider. While the house carries a pulled-together air of sophistication, it's equally approachable—like an old friend. You can walk into the sunroom and put your feet up on the coffee table that doubles as an ottoman. You can sink into the cut-velvet chairs in the formal living room. All of these elements speak to elegance without the fuss of formality.

Early on in the process, the owners said to me, "We trust you completely—make the design your signature." What a compliment! Not only was I able to use bold color and pattern but also cherished antiques and heirlooms to make the home a unique reflection of their taste and histories.

Textures tell a tale in every room, and there's something about contrast that makes a design sing. To find that perfect balance, I like to layer different textures and patterns like the cut-velvet geometric on the stools, the Chinese dragon print on the ottoman, and the zebra-inspired stripe on the wingback chair in this living room.

Whether for function or just to catch the eye, every room needs a metal. I like pairing shiny metal accents with matte finishes. For example, this powder room's wallpaper has both matte and shimmer stripes that juxtapose so effortlessly with the finish on the vanity's metal legs, frames, and picture lights.

Shiny gold or chrome accents pair brilliantly with stone, brick, or rock in a kitchen, creating a mix of porous and shiny. In this room, a serpent mirror was an unexpected way to add some polish against the neutral solid-surface backsplash.

A high-gloss paint in your favorite color on mudroom
walls makes for a happy entrance into the home.

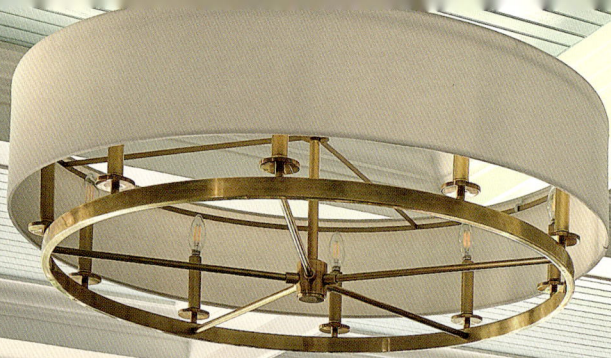

Grass cloth and lacquer offer an unexpected pairing. I like to cover wall or ceiling spaces with grass cloth and then add some shine with a lacquer on the trim or cabinetry. The tray ceilings in these rooms worked particularly well for the rough, scratchy wallpaper, while the walls shine in a teal lacquer.

A whimsical orange wallpaper paired with a traditional acrylic-and-brass leg vanity is an easy mix of fresh and classic in this bath.

As the saying goes, "If it's not moving, monogram it!" There are few things I deem more Southern than a monogram. It's an elegant way of displaying your family heritage. Bedding is a natural place for a monogram, whether you choose to embroider the shams, duvet, sheets, or an accent pillow. Square Euro shams make a great background for a two-letter monogram. If you have a king-sized bed, plan for three pillows to fill the space adequately.

# 2

# OLD and NEW

CREATING PATINA

As Southerners, we're all about heritage. We want to know everyone's and everything's backstory; like whose great-aunt a piece once belonged to and how you've turned it into something you now use all the time. In our homes, nothing says heritage quite like a piece that has a little age or patina to it—or at least looks like it does. Whether you live in a 100-year-old Colonial that also happens to be where your grandparents raised their children or are in the process of building a new home and starting your own traditions, there are so many ways to bring in generational additions that are also realistic for how we live today.

One of my favorite ways to make a home's patina stand out is to highlight features that are timeless or maybe even a bit special because you don't see them in every corner, like a brass weather vane, a copper lantern with a bit of verdigris, or even a handsome sideboard that's been in service for centuries. Sometimes—and most definitely when we are adding on or building fresh—I need to put those elements into place to make the house look and feel like it's evolved through the years. A good way to do this is by using materials that have stood the test of time and selecting applications or techniques that are also ageless. For example, a marble shower wall that is laid in a herringbone pattern or paneling that makes architectural art out of formerly blank walls. If we're speaking in absolutes, design elements like wood or brick floors, grass cloth wallcoverings or scenic murals, and wall sconces or picture lights always bring intrigue and will never go out of style. It's finding a way to incorporate that little something that causes you to pause and say, "Wait, I thought they just built this house."

Outside of architectural features, art and antiques are my go-tos for creating an instant sense of patina. When you incorporate a collection of art, china, or silver that you have thoughtfully curated over time, it's noticeable and can be a conversation starter. It goes back to that innate Southern curiosity and desire to know where you got a piece and what you love about it. In short, these collections tell a bit of your story. The same is true for antiques. I love it when clients own a beloved dining table or buffet they inherited and want to continue to use with future generations. But equally fun is shopping for an antique piece that suits their style and will function well for them.

While patina brings a level of interest, I never want that to overpower the home, making it feel dated or rendering it nonfunctional. To keep it fresh, I turn back to color, bold fabrics, and inviting upholstered pieces. I also think about the details and how they contribute to the overall design. For example, I like to add traditional built-ins with panel-front doors but then top them off with modern hardware. Or conversely, I might pair abstract art with brass, classic-lined picture lights. It truly is the mix of old and new that keeps a design interesting.

# DRAPER ONE

This home has a storied history that began with two notable craftsmen and artisans—both of whose impacts reached far beyond the borders of the Commonwealth of Virginia. Clinton Harriman Cowgill founded Virginia Tech's architecture department and served as its head for almost thirty years. He not only taught but also designed campus buildings and several Blacksburg Historic Structures—including this home. He worked with John W. Whittemore, who restored much of Colonial Williamsburg, to build. It is the owners' understanding that the oversized exterior bricks for the original house were made on site, resembling the ones you would see today at Colonial Williamsburg. We definitely weren't touching those treasures!

I wanted to play up all the historical aspects of this 1936 home with decor and finishes that would continue to build on its patina. The previous owners had added on a breakfast room, but I added the brick-look tile and laid it in a very timeless herringbone pattern. I also added paneling, which gives the space some architectural bones and meshes well with the original portion of the home. The paneling was carried through into the kitchen as well. To make the banquette look original to the home, we added the circular window that is more native to 1930s structures than it is to today's builds. We also installed an arched window in the kitchen. These new features make the house feel like it has been in place for decades.

The silver perched on the newly added shelving gives another layer of age. It's a simple, cosmetic way to bring in some character, and the shelves makes it easy for the couple—who entertain frequently—to walk into the room and gather what they need with ease. When they host, they love to use their sterling flatware and fine dinnerware, thus I wanted everything to be accessible.

Of course, I put my signature spin on the design with color, fabrics, and art. A warm, inviting red works nicely in the den and adjoining bar area. Pieces from their original art collection are placed throughout the house. Other subtle touches, such as the custom teal table base by Dunes and Duchess in the breakfast nook and the large-scale pendants over the kitchen island, add layering.

At the front door, they have a mail slot—which again highlights the home's original era. We complemented this with a silver tray where they might place the day's mail, grass cloth on the walls, and a more contemporary light fixture and pillow fabrics. It creates that back-and-forth dance between having ageless, time-honored elements while keeping your home fresh with colors and accessories that are of today.

The patterned shades on the window seat's swing-arm sconces play
well with the other fabrics in the room and the overall palette.

Leaving no space unused, I put pattern on the chairs, underfoot on the rug, and even on the ceiling in the form of a multihued wallpaper. The overall effect is a symphony of prints that brings a sense of evolved-over-time character.

In the kitchen, I added a new arched window that looks as if it could have been original to the home, furthering the updated room's patina. The window's classic shape highlights the millwork that frames it; the modern articulating faucet becomes a focal point.

The shelves above the breakfast banquette hold inherited silver platters, an easy way to give a room instant patina. They mix with more current yet classic blue Ginori dishes, displaying the best of past and present.

# 3

# TO the WALLS

## WALLPAPER AND PAINT

In terms of impact, few elements rank higher on the design list than wallpaper and paint. Perhaps because they are given so much square footage, wallpaper and paint can instantly set a mood, making them a hugely important part of a home's overall scheme. The touch of a paintbrush or a roll of wallpaper can create a bold statement or a serene retreat. I like to think about color theory, or the way colors make you feel, when I'm designing a space. For example, red can be warm, inviting, and dramatic, making it an excellent choice for gathering spaces, while light yellow and soft pinks can feel calming and invite relaxation, rest, and peace, making them ideal for bedrooms and baths.

Personally, I am drawn to cobalt blue and cornflower blue, shades of orange, and kelly green, and they make frequent appearances in my work. When I'm looking to use more calming, lighter tones, I often choose a combination of light blue and white, khaki, or camel. To give the same effect with wallpaper, it can be as simple as selecting something that doesn't have a lot of pattern but uses texture to bring interest, such as a timeless grass cloth.

If you've seen any of my work—or flipped through the pages of this book—you may have gathered that it's not really in our vocabulary to do solely neutral rooms! I tend to think of colors such as the light blue I just mentioned as being neutral. Sometimes a color will function as a neutral when it fills an entire room: it becomes a part of the backdrop, the furnishings, and the accessories, creating a sense of continuity for the eye.

It takes confidence and a certain level of comfort to take on the challenge of using strong color. Sometimes when I meet with a client, I find that they have hired me to help them come around to color and figure out how to use it more boldly, particularly on their walls. Often, when given a little encouragement and direction, they will embrace bright hues and love how they can be used to bring their house to life. For instance, we have a client who was very into neutrals—everything was beige and gray—but I've given her confidence with color in her primary residence, and she fully embraced it in their second home. She is even more confident with color in her wardrobe now, too!

One way I like to start building that confidence is by finding a piece of art, fabric, or a rug that the client loves and pulling just one color from it for the walls. It's not overwhelming to start in that vein, and it's encouraging to see something you like applied in a different manner and on a larger scale.

Outside of the colors selected for wall paint, there's also the finish to consider. I love to use high-gloss paint if the walls are new or in excellent shape. For older homes, if natural light tends to highlight the wall's slight imperfections, I recommend using a classic eggshell finish that won't make those stand out. Adding paneling in an older home can help break up the expanse and then add the lacquered look. In either case, leave it to a pro. High-gloss application is not a do-it-yourself project.

# LONGVIEW

When you step into this Roanoke, Virginia, residence there's an air of femininity that greets you at the front door. Yet two teenage boys and their father also feel right at home in this classic Federal-style house. While the design really embraces the mother's love of color, it also has very tailored, masculine qualities that keep it balanced.

The family of four had been debating a move but loved their location and the overall footprint of the house. That's when they called me to update the interiors and make it their dream home. Built in 1925, the structure is understated and unpresuming, which is one of my favorite things about it. The family let me do my magic, immediately signing off on our initial presentation. Because they were ready for something entirely different, we brought in almost all new furnishings. However, they had a fabulous art collection, which they kept; it was used as the source of inspiration for much of the color throughout the spaces. If you purchase great art, it's going to work somewhere, it's just a matter of being able to reposition and incorporate pieces throughout the rooms. For example, the teal for the living room comes from a pair of portraits of the boys.

Without changing the structure of the home, and thinking about how the family lives at this stage of life, we were also able to redefine some of the rooms. The biggest change was in swapping the placement of their living and dining rooms to allow for a larger, more comfortable space where everyone could hang out, watch sports, play games, and just be together. The darker, rich teal color pulled from the portraits made the entire space feel inviting and warm, a place where you just want to curl up and relax.

This house didn't really have a foyer, so in reworking the dining room I also added a banquette at the front door. It's a perfect little nook for greeting guests with a predinner

I painted the shutters and front door of this home in Benjamin Moore "Palladium Blue," as a subtle, not-so-intense way to give it some color, and—just as importantly—to introduce a hue that you'll also see inside. The same color makes an appearance on the interior side of the entry door and the banister, thus connecting the outdoors to the inside with a single paint swatch.

cocktail or just a great spot to unwind with a book. Here, rather than paint we used a
fabulous Scalamandré wallpaper with a chinoiserie bamboo fretwork design. It still
brings color but gives the room a bit of a dressier look and differentiates it from the den
across the hall, creating two distinct spaces for the family to host others and to enjoy
time together.

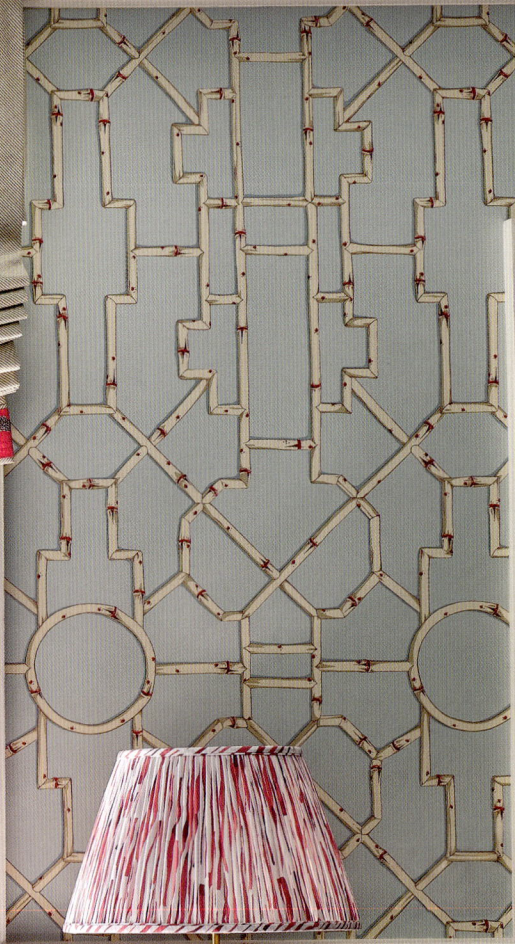

Opposite the front door, this end of the dining room has an intimate nook for the family piano. The Scalamandré bamboo-fretwork wallpaper carries throughout the entire space and pairs with the chinoiserie window treatments. Rather than use a wooden piano bench, I had a little fun with the fuchsia X bench that is the perfect height.

Family portraits were the starting and focal points for the living room. I wanted them to pop so I brought in pattern on the ceiling and the rug and kept the walls a solid teal hue. The timeless frame molding stands out thanks to the lacquer finish.

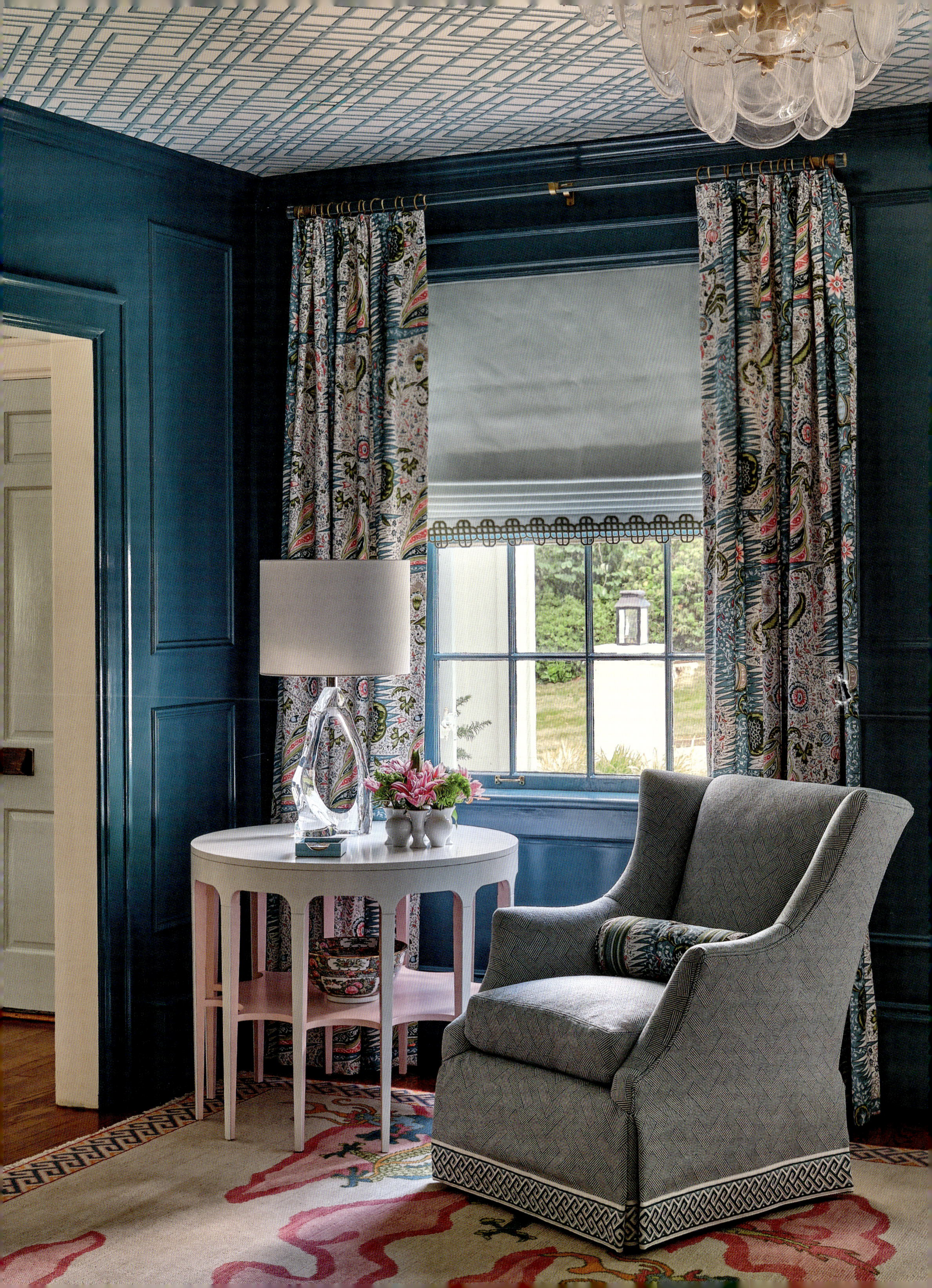

From the living room, you catch a glimpse of the breakfast nook's magenta fretwork wallpaper. Visually, it ties into both the dragon-embellished rug here and the dining room's bamboo wallpaper.

In a central area of the home, we did a light refresh on the bar, trading a tile backsplash for a punched-up pink grass cloth and adding hardware that looks like jewelry against the white cabinetry.

# 4

# The FIFTH WALL

SHOWCASING CEILINGS WITH STYLE

When I start to design a room, I am always looking up. The fifth wall, or the ceiling, is a canvas that can be overlooked, neglected, or covered with a coat of neutral paint and forgotten, but not in my book. I like to use every square inch of space, and that most definitely includes the ceiling. I typically choose one of three paths: paint it in an accent color, cover it with wallpaper, or apply a millwork treatment.

Several factors come into play when deciding which option to use. First, as always, I think of my rule of mixing geometrics, florals, and solids to see what might be missing in this space. I also think about how much drama this room needs or does not need. This is where I look at the surrounding walls and adjacent rooms and really put that formula to the test in terms of how the space will not only look, but also feel, when you walk into it. Maybe it's a dining room that can incorporate a wallpaper with a bit more flair. Or, perhaps, you want to invite calm with a soft hue on a bedroom ceiling.

When I choose to paint the fifth wall, I love to pull an accent color from a wallpaper, fabric, or a rug and then take it upward. It's an unexpected yet very sensible way to carry a palette throughout a room and make every surface feel like it's been thoughtfully designed. If the home has been recently built or renovated and has ceilings that are in excellent shape and won't show imperfections, I often like to do a high-gloss finish that gives a polished feel.

In older homes or places where a ceiling is not in peak shape, I love the thought of using grass cloth. Its texture will hide imperfections and blemishes. You can bring in that accent thread or choose a metallic finish if you want a look that is more neutral and quiet. When opting for a patterned paper on the ceiling, I think about its direction as well as any angles that might be present. For example, you wouldn't want a garden or pastoral print that seems to "grow" from the ground up covering the ceiling. Similarly, a lattice or plaid could create an unwanted optical illusion if there are numerous angles. For rooms that are an odd shape, florals and solids are always a safe bet.

Last, but certainly not least, adding a three-dimensional millwork treatment to a ceiling is one of my favorite ways to create architectural interest. Millwork can be painted along with the rest of the ceiling in an accent color or with a classic white, following suit with the rest of the trim to frame the entire room. This is such a simple yet thoughtful way to give even a newly built home instant age or patina, especially if you use a timeless pattern such as a Chippendale or fretwork motif.

# PALMETTO 25

When this young family of five moved to South Carolina, they were ready to make a
completely fresh start with their interiors. After they purchased a house that was built
in 2000, we embarked on a full, down-to-the-studs renovation to create a home with
character where the couple could entertain and the children could grow. For starters,
I embraced color (as I always do!) while being mindful that the wife also liked neutrals. Performance fabrics and easy-to-clean wool rugs were used throughout the house
so they could really live here. We also gave the home a bit of soul with a few furnishings
that didn't necessarily look new and by adding some timeless architectural features.

The renovation started outside where red brick was painted in a more toned-down
cream, and the front door and planters introduced the blue hue that continues indoors.
However, the entire thread for the design started with a fabulous scenic Schumacher
wallpaper that I knew was perfect for the dining room. I used the wallpaper's blush
background color on the ceiling in a high-gloss finish and  completed the look with a
French chandelier. I love creating the contrast between the matte scenic wallpaper and
the luminescent ceiling. With candlelight at night, it really makes it magical. I was also
able to play off the blues and greens in the wallpaper to come up with a palette for the
adjoining spaces; in fact, that's where the blue for the entry door got its start.

When thinking about how to give this home a bit more architectural interest, the
fifth wall of the living room and entry stair walls were two places that seemed to be
natural fits. We added molding to create paneled walls on previously blank spaces in
the entry. This draws the eye up and showcases the grandness of the foyer along with
its curved staircase. Additionally, this space flows into the living room where we used a

similar treatment on the ceiling. Previously, this was a two-story room. We brought the ceiling down, which allowed for the creation of a bunk room upstairs and gave us the opportunity to add a simple Chippendale pattern. We kept this millwork white to match the room's trim. The rest of the space is drenched in blue, giving it plenty of drama on its own and letting a commissioned diptych of the couple's favorite Kiawah Island view shine. It's a space that reads elegant and sophisticated but is still casual enough for easy conversation, making it a perfect stopping point when guests enter the house.

The kitchen, breakfast area, and family room all have a more neutral background, but the same thread of blue makes a big statement on the range hood. For continuity, this color also appears alongside green in the draperies and on furnishings and pillows. Dining and coffee tables in cerused and pickled wood finishes hold up to the wear and tear of daily life and give a casual feel in these more private spaces.

The handsome study is a bit of a departure from this color scheme but for good reason. It pays homage to the schools where the husband has served as a college football coach. The walls are covered with a brown-based grass cloth that uses garnet wax rivets to create a stately square pattern, while the leading edge of the draperies has a coordinating tape. The art here is a very sentimental, special duo: in the piece on the left, he is depicted standing on the field with his dad years ago, in the piece on the right, he is shown, years later, with his own son in almost exactly the same stance on another field. The wife had these pieces commissioned from artist Kelly Pelfrey and gifted them to her husband. His parents were given copies, and I love to think about the little cries of joy on Christmas morning when they opened them. It is a sweet memory to look back on as they continue to make new memories in this classic home.

The dining room's Schumacher wallpaper was the starting point for the room's design and palette. To keep it feeling fresh, I pulled the thread of pink onto the ceiling in a high-gloss finish.

When a bookcase is painted in a bright color, I love to introduce a
scratchy, neutral grass cloth for its backing and contrast that with
shiny hardware.

When the couple purchased the home, the living room had a vaulted ceiling. We lowered it to create a bunk room upstairs, giving us the opportunity to add a ceiling treatment. I wanted it to have some age and patina, so I chose a Chippendale millwork pattern. It adds just enough interest to the ceiling without overpowering the room. The commissioned diptych is a view on Kiawah Island, a favorite vacation spot for this couple.

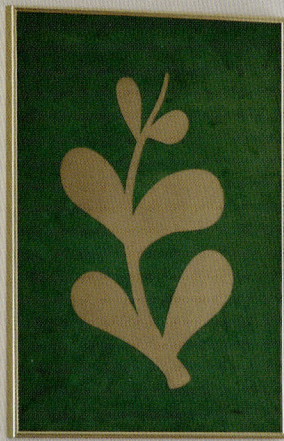

In the family room, I pulled the room's green hue onto the back of the built-ins. Adding a bright color or wallpaper to the back of a bookcase is one of my favorite ways to create a custom look.

Rather than adding more concealed cabinetry, I opted for a set of bistro shelves between the paneled refrigerator and freezer. They bring in a metal element that plays off the patina in the room's mirrors and also provides a focal point, which I filled with decorative and textured items like the wicker baskets and boxwoods.

We went dramatic with this beverage center backsplash that features a shapely, yet classic design paired with antiqued mirrors.

BEAUTY AT HOME   AERIN LAUDER

Entertaining Chic! Modern French Recipes & Table Settings for All Occasions   Claudia Pontigny

SCOTT SHRADER   THE ART OF OUTDOOR LIVING

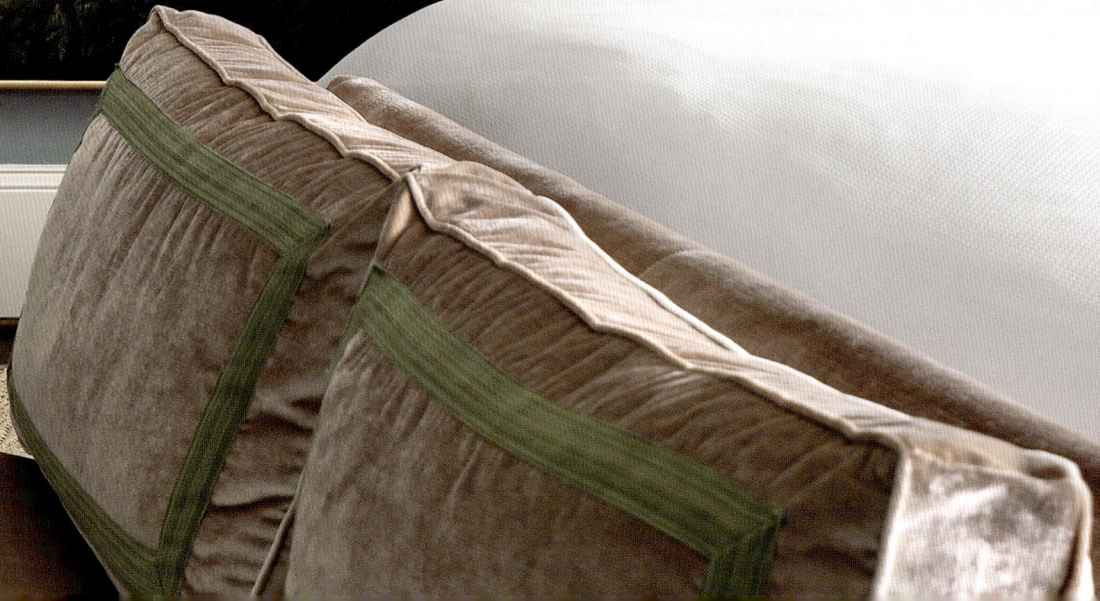

In the primary bedroom, I used a series of sheer panels across the back wall to soften the burled wood chests and create a slightly dramatic statement behind the bed. A second diptych of a marsh scene echoes the look of the family room.

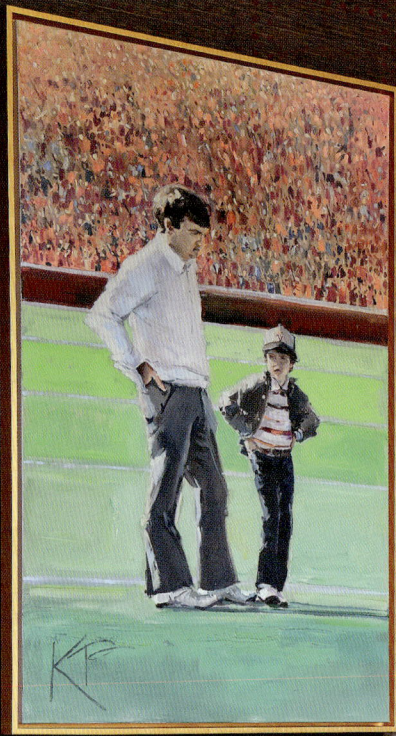

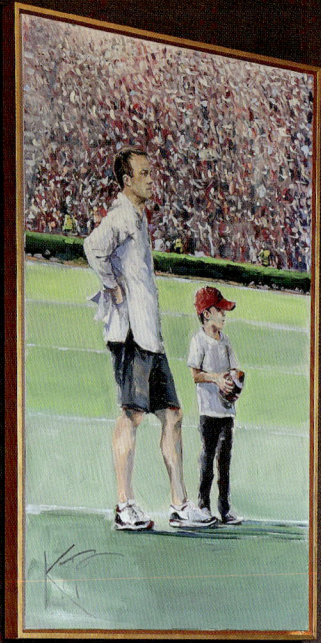

The chocolate and garnet palette in the gentleman's study is a bit
of a departure from the rest of the house, giving it a destination
feel. Artist Kelly Pelfrey, who I work with frequently, created the
pair of father-son portraits, which depict three generations.

Adjacent to the mudroom, this powder room is in a high-traffic area. I kept it very practical with a brick floor and woven shades but still dressed it up with a whimsical Schumacher wallpaper and large hardware centered on the cabinet fronts.

In the main powder room, I pulled in a Lee Jofa wallpaper that complements the wallcovering in the dining room. The same pink used on that room's ceiling also appears on the baseboards and ceiling in this space to create a feeling of continuity for guests.

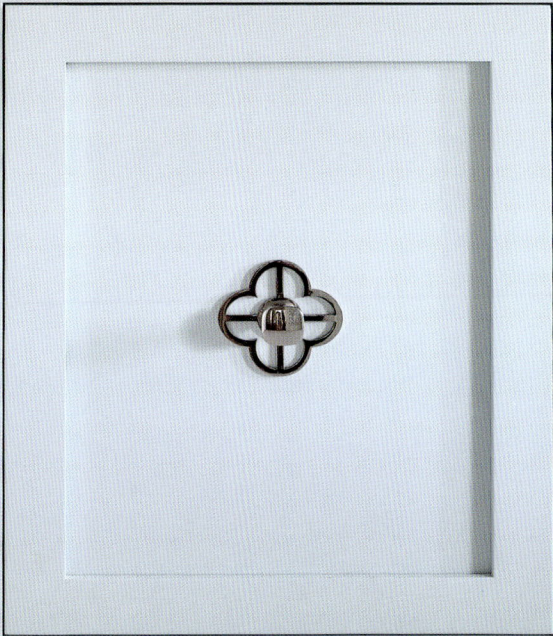

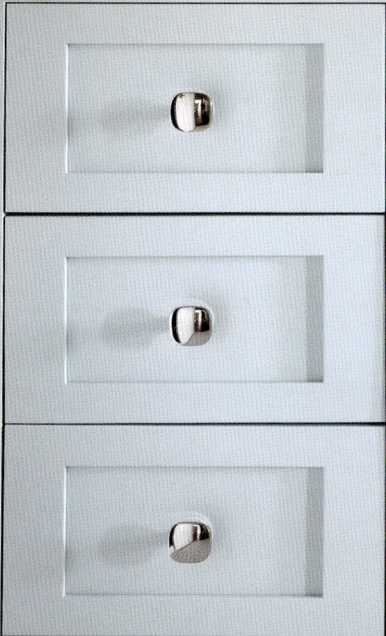

# 5

# ART SMART

SELECTING AND DISPLAYING WORKS

When I think of art in a home, I think of personalization. Often, some of the most meaningful items we own are art. At some point, the paintings, sculptures, and photographs that fill our walls and stand on our entry pieces spoke to us—and continue to do so. It might be a memento you picked up from a street vendor when you were in New Orleans or Nice. It could be a photograph you took on a particularly memorable beach trip with loved ones. Perhaps it's an idyllic landscape watercolor you first saw in a gallery window that now gives you peace each time you round the corner and catch a glimpse of it. Or it could possibly even be a framed menu you chose to keep following an especially delightful dinner with friends.

Personally, I collect paintings of dogs, and I'm always on the hunt for these when I travel or browse my favorite stores. Not only do I love pups, but it's also fun to hunt for a certain item that will fit into my collection. I continue to add to this grouping as I come across pieces I am drawn to and as my budget allows—a philosophy that anyone can put into practice when it comes to collecting art.

Collecting and artfully displaying works that bring us joy is a natural way to ensure we're creating spaces we love. For this reason, art plays a significant role in my work as a designer. It's about capturing a feeling and being instantly transported back to it each time you enter a room or look at a specific piece—a reflective practice that is at the heart of being Southern.

Aside from the personal aspects, there's another practical element about art in our interiors: it can be a fabulous starting point for a room's design. If a client brings me an abstract piece they want to use in their den, I'll immediately start pulling fabric swatches that work with its palette and feel. If they have family portraits to display in a study, I begin to think about their frames and the overall symphony of finishes we'll use. Because of their beauty and their owners' emotional attachment, I love to give these pieces a prominent place and build a room around them.

In terms of display, I believe in going big and choosing prominent, highly visible spaces to make an impact. In the same way that I enjoy playing with color and creating a thread throughout a home, I also like to highlight scenes and pieces that are reflective of the client. For example, landscape or botanical murals that are a nod to the client's heritage or that are customized to include their favorite birds can make for a beautiful backdrop in a dining room. Focal points over a fireplace or bed are oftentimes prime real estate for an aptly placed single painting or series of smaller watercolors.

When I'm helping clients select art, I often suggest a commission—especially if they have a certain space to fill and we're not finding just the thing that speaks to them. I like to support local artists, and I don't use mass-produced pieces in my work. To begin this process, I ask my client to think of a photograph from a special trip, place, or event or ask them to take pictures of items and scenes they are drawn to—even if they aren't sure what it is that attracts them. The artist can use all of this information to create a piece meant only for that homeowner. As a designer, I'll find the perfect place for it to live within the home.

# EAST LANDING

Moving to eastern Virginia to be closer to her children and grandchildren, this client purchased a home in a highly traditional, classic colonial town. We set out to update the house, which was built in 1996, while giving it character and a bit of age. Playing to both the setting and her personality, murals and commissioned pieces were used prominently in the overall design.

This starts as you enter the home and come into a grand combination living and dining space where a mural from Schumacher's Iksel collaboration fills the walls. The room is so large that the mural almost wraps around you. If it were a solid color, it would be imposing, but here you have the comfort of the trees in scale. That's how I knew the mural was the perfect choice. When working with murals, I keep the aperture of view in mind. As long as you have the ground in view and the majority of the top of the scene, you can keep the scale correct. The owner has a collection of Canton porcelain that coordinates beautifully with this particular bucolic scene. It shows up on the garden stool, along the mantel, and in the china cabinet, giving the room a traditional flair; geometric chairs and a bamboo acrylic side table keep it fresh.

For the commissioned pieces, we worked with South Carolina artist Kelly Pelfrey. Years ago, I saw one of Kelly's pieces on Instagram and fell in love with her classic, loose, fresh style. She has no fear of color, and she really understands my aesthetic and can capture and translate it so well.

In the blue-and-white breakfast nook, we needed a prominent piece for an angled wall that faces the kitchen and the entrance to this space. We talked about the palette, the use of the room, and the fact that we wanted fruit and flowers to be a part of the still

life. As I always do, I sent Kelly swatches to get an exact match. As a final personal touch, we decided to nestle the homeowner's Juliska pattern into the painting, leaving no doubt that this was the room and the person for whom this piece was made.

In the sunroom, the client asked us to use a photograph she took of a koi pond as inspiration. We worked with Kelly and she turned the photograph into a painting, which I then placed in a very current gallery frame over the mantel. We pulled the colors for the rest of the room from the lily pad leaves and brought in a casual rattan credenza and an Aerin Lauder floral chandelier overhead, all of which create a storied, feminine space that is perfectly reflective of its owner.

A light blush hue reigns in the primary bedroom. A high-gloss paint and geometric rug provide a contemporary balance against the floral fabric and shapely valance and settee. We wanted this space to be extra feminine but it's also a fun and inviting place for her to hang out with her grandchildren. The art on the mantel repeats back all of the colors in the space.

Many times when I begin working with a client they will bring special paintings or portraits they want to use in the design of the home. To modernize the pieces or make them fit purposefully into the scheme, I will have them reframed or hang them in a nontraditional manner. In the study, two portraits of the client's grandparents' homes were important, sentimental pieces she wanted to display. I modernized these by hanging them on mirrors, an unexpected way to make them stand out in the room while also giving them a bit of levity. It's a way of incorporating a traditional Southern element while pushing the envelope a bit.

Art is so deeply personal but when a commissioned piece can incorporate something unique to an individual, it becomes even more so. The piece on this sidewall features the very breakfast dishes and vase that are used in this room.

I love to drench a space in the same hue to create a little jewel box
that is accented with patterned fabrics, rugs, and, of course, art.

This wallpaper and window treatment grouping is a great example of my philosophy of pairing a small print or solid with a botanical and a geometric pattern—it's a formula that never fails!

# 6

# COLOR RULES
# to LIVE BY

CREATING A PALETTE

It's no secret that color is life-giving to me. I think this started at an early age. Each summer, my grandmother, Nancy (I had to call her by her first name—not "Grandmother" or "Nana"), would take me shopping at The Cricket Shop in Pawleys Island, South Carolina, which featured Lilly Pulitzer. If you're familiar with the brand, you know that pinks, greens, and yellows in patterns galore are its calling card, and I was in love. From then on, I have always been drawn to color for my wardrobe, and it was natural for it to show up in a big way in my work.

There are two principles I use in every project I touch when it comes to incorporating color. First, I start the color story as soon as possible. Sometimes, this means that even before you set foot in the house, you have already picked up on the palette, taking cues from the shutters or the front door that are painted in a hue you're sure to see inside. Other times, the thread starts in the entry. Whatever I'm using as the main colors throughout the design are introduced here, letting you know what to expect as you move deeper into the house. It might be a fabulous blue-and-white table skirt on a console that signals the start of the scheme. Or it could be a wallcovering that has hints of pink you'll see in adjoining rooms. Whatever the selection, it's so important to give guests an introduction to the color palette of a house in this way.

Second, I follow something I like to call the "Three Color Rule." The principle of grouping objects in sets of three is nothing new, but I apply it specifically to color. As mentioned, I'll start a thread with the home's main hue in the entry but the supporting colors will be there as well. If I use blue as an accent at the front door, you can bet you'll see blue in one of the entry's adjoining rooms—possibly as the main color—along with two other colors, such as green and yellow. Leading further into the house, the next room could be predominantly green with blue and yellow as its accents. I like to pulse those different colors within a palette throughout a house yet always keep a common thread that feels familiar. I'll still pop in an orange book or a painting with pink and purple here and there, but the overall palette is found in the paint scheme, furniture, fabrics, and rugs. Keeping your palette to three colors is an easy-to-remember guideline that can simplify a design. Plus, being able to tie at least one of those colors to a corresponding space creates cohesion for the eye—even if you don't expressly pick up on it.

# BRIERYLE BY THE JAMES

I designed this house in Richmond for a young family who were willing to be bold
with their color selections. Built in 1950, it's an older, endearing home with a timeless
white German smear brick and black shutters on the exterior. Due to its era, the interior
already had a traditional flair they appreciated, but we wanted to make it feel very livable
and sensible for a family with young children. To blend these classic elements with color,
it felt natural to give the home a bit of a preppy essence by incorporating plaid and
collegiate-stripe pieces. We even went with an orange palette in some of the gathering
spaces as a nod to the couple's days at the University of Virginia.

Following my own color rules, I started by introducing blue—which is seen throughout the house—in the entry. It shows up in the blue-and-white, Chippendale-patterned
wallpaper and on the ginger jars, rug, and chair fabric. Curated, timeless elements like
an older French-style mirror and cachepot are mixed with a more modern-shaped
credenza that still has a traditional feel thanks to its mahogany wood.

The dining and living rooms are on respective sides of the entry, allowing me to
deftly introduce a couple of new hues that play off the blue in the foyer. In the dining
room, it's green. All the millwork, a key architectural element, was highlighted with a
high-gloss green while the ceiling was painted pale blue and the walls covered in a floral
paper. The entire room is saturated in color! The blue-and-white you saw in the foyer
shows up in a big way on this room's rug, but green is still the star here. We balanced the
inherited pedestal table with more contemporary white loop side chairs, comfortable
upholstered host chairs, and a modern light fixture. This room is so inviting. To me, it
says, "Come gather here, sit down, and enjoy yourself."

Across the hall, green becomes the accent color with blue and white along with pops of yellow taking center stage. The lemon-themed Schumacher fabric was the starting point of this space, but outside of that everything is covered in a hue of blue. The couple wanted a softer, airier feel in this room so we chose a lighter blue wall color and then mixed in the darker navy furnishings and rug. This room is such a good example of choosing a starting point you love (like the fabric here) and then allowing the design to flow from there.

Deeper into the house, the family room, kitchen, and breakfast room are all connected in an open layout. We made them feel cohesive with a whimsical Cole & Son wallpaper that features playful monkeys alongside elegant persimmons. In the family room, a madras plaid-style rug brings the same color combo to the floor that's also dotted around the room in the cabinetry paint, window treatments, and pillows. All of these pieces not only adhere to my color mantra, but also to my philosophy of incorporating a floral, a geometric, and a solid within a room's design.

In the primary bedroom, blue shrinks to a small accent, showing up in a collection of blue-and-white pieces that include bedside lamps, a garden stool, and a ginger jar. The overscaled Christopher Farr drapery fabric was the genesis of this room, accented with a smaller Schumacher pattern on the bed that is in the same color family. Two big structural changes made this space work better for the family's day-to-day use and style. First, we updated a built-in shelving unit that was likely original to the home with a chinoiserie design I sketched and filled it with collected pieces they already owned. Second, because this is an older home it lacked closet space. The shape of the long rectangular room allowed us to take one wall to create a dressing closet, making the space as functional as it is fashionable.

As the main color in the foyer, blue shows up in the bamboo fretwork wallpaper, the rug, and the accessories. To create a visual trail for the eye, I pulled that thread into the dining room as an accent color against the bold green paint.

On the other side of the foyer, across from the dining room, we fully leaned into blue. The room is drenched in a harmonious blend of different shades that are accented with a bit of green and yellow—in the form of a cheerful lemon-print fabric.

Deeper into the home, one of the most used spaces is a combination living and dining area. It pairs blue with orange—a nod to the couple's University of Virginia roots—and is playfully preppy thanks to a collegiate plaid rug and wallpaper featuring mischievous monkeys.

The color palette changes in the primary bedroom, signaling that it is a more private, set-apart destination. The Christopher Farr fabric on the window treatment started the scheme for this space, making shades of purple and pink the focus with green and blue showing up as accents.

I think it's so important for kids' rooms to be able to grow with the child. The girl this room belongs to was a preteen when we selected the Gray Malin "Pool Day, The Beverly Hills Hotel" photograph as the starting point for her space. It and the whimsical window treatment fabric keep the space feeling girlish yet sophisticated.

# 7

# CREATING HARMONY

BALANCE, REPETITION, AND SCALE

It's natural to see a fabric, a piece of furniture, or a light fixture and think, "I love that, I'll find a spot for it." If you really love it, then the adage is true—you will find the perfect place. But how do you make all of these finds work together in your home in a balanced, eye-pleasing fashion? While the eye itself can be a fabulous indicator, I like to use a bit of math as well.

I have a formula I employ when it comes to textiles, wallcoverings, and rugs or flooring. It's a sensible approach involving a simple equation that won't steer you wrong. The elements it includes are classic Southern staples, including geometric, floral, and plaid or stripe prints, along with solid colors. One is the statement piece or star and the others will play a supporting role. Not surprisingly, you go big with the star and let the others fill in the space with a complementary position.

Scale is also immensely important in this mix. If the star is a large geometric, then I choose a smaller floral, check, or a solid to pair with it. Two prints in the same style can also go together if they are different in scale—for example, a big, blossoming botanical on the walls and a smaller floral on a side chair. It's all in thinking about how to bring life to the space without overpowering it. Not only is the scale of the print important, the overall scale or size of the room needs to be considered. In a room with tall ceilings, a wallcovering print that fills the expanse is a good choice; a small pattern could feel too delicate and diminish the grandness of the space.

Just as I consider scale, I also take into account balance and repetition. If an accent wall is covered in a standout green paper, you'll want to see a variation of that green elsewhere in the room to keep it from feeling off-kilter. This goes for finishes, too. It's not necessary to be matchy-matchy, selecting only one finish throughout a room, but it is important to think about things like where to use brushed brass and where to bring in chrome to give a cohesive look. Thoughtfully approaching questions of balance and repetition can result in a curated look that seems to have evolved over time, and it's another subtle way to create a custom home.

Repeating colors is a classic way to tie a room together, and repeating motifs has the same effect. Patterns can be accented with light fixtures, fabric tapes and trims, accessories, or furnishings that carry the thread throughout the room. It could be a bamboo light fixture that echoes the chinoiserie wallpaper, a charming shade of coral that is pulled from a rug, or fretwork that appears on a chair back and repeats on the window treatment fabric. In essence, every element of design has a family it belongs to and these are placed throughout the room, making it easy for the eye to create connections and see a well-balanced beauty.

# AVENHAM

I love a good surprise, and the way the purchase of this house unfolded was definitely a surprise—at least for one of the owners, as her husband gave her the deed on Christmas morning. She had long admired the home, which was built in 1914 on a charming street in Roanoke's historic district. She was thrilled to have the keys, and I was thrilled to help them renovate and repair the structure to make it more current and functional.

During its heyday, the house played host to grand parties and community events. The couple wanted to restore some of this former glory but in a way that felt inviting, approachable, and not at all pretentious. Sometimes when I do an initial site visit, I will jokingly report that the home has "osteoporosis." However, that was not the case here. The bones of the house were fabulous, and I knew I could accentuate them with well-placed doses of color.

Because it is a large home, there were multiple opportunities to bring in pattern and emphasize the tall ceilings and gracious rooms, while being respectful of its heritage. I started this endeavor by painting the front door a vivid teal, as a sort of introduction to what you'll see when stepping into the oversized foyer, where a fabric using the same hue covers a console table. Following my pattern formula, I used a large-scale acanthus stripe wallpaper that draws the eye up and also repeats on a similar feathery element of the chandelier. Next, the side chairs were covered in a small-scale geometric gros point and cut-velvet upholstery fabric. It's hard to grasp just how big this room is but for reference the orchid stands at five feet tall!

As you continue further into the house, the family room has an intentionally symmetrical design. The fireplace was a focal point so both the left and right side needed to

be balanced with furniture placement and accessories. Here, a large-scale trellis paper on the walls works well with a repeated small geometric pattern on the sofa, with green at all points. Because the room is so big, we also broke it up by creating a separate nook for a game table. The teal from the entry is pulled in through pillows and accessories, creating a common thread for the eye.

As one of the most utilitarian spaces in any home, the kitchen is a place you might not expect to see pattern—but if you know me, I'll find a way. We opened up the former dining room to create one large kitchen that has a separate cozy dining area (which is perfect for these empty nesters to enjoy on nights alone) as well as a roomy desk area. Both of these spaces have a cheerful yellow geometric wallcovering that sets the tone. In the cooking area, one long wall really needed to have its own presence. For this I created a shapely solid-surface backsplash behind the eight-burner range. It's graceful, easy to clean, and perfectly balanced by a set of bistro shelves on either side. Again, that warm, rich teal hue makes an appearance to keep it from feeling cold and to tie all of the gathering spaces together.

In the dining room, we used green in much the same way many would use a neutral—by placing it everywhere. With a solid focal point on the bookcases, botanical print on the drapes, and a rug with a smaller print, all the elements work together in harmony.

The breakfast nook and office that adjoin the kitchen get a ton of use. Because the family spends so much time here, we wanted it to be a statement room. We went big with the trellis wallpaper and geometric light fixture over the table and repeated the botanical fabric on the windows and banquette for familiarity throughout the large space.

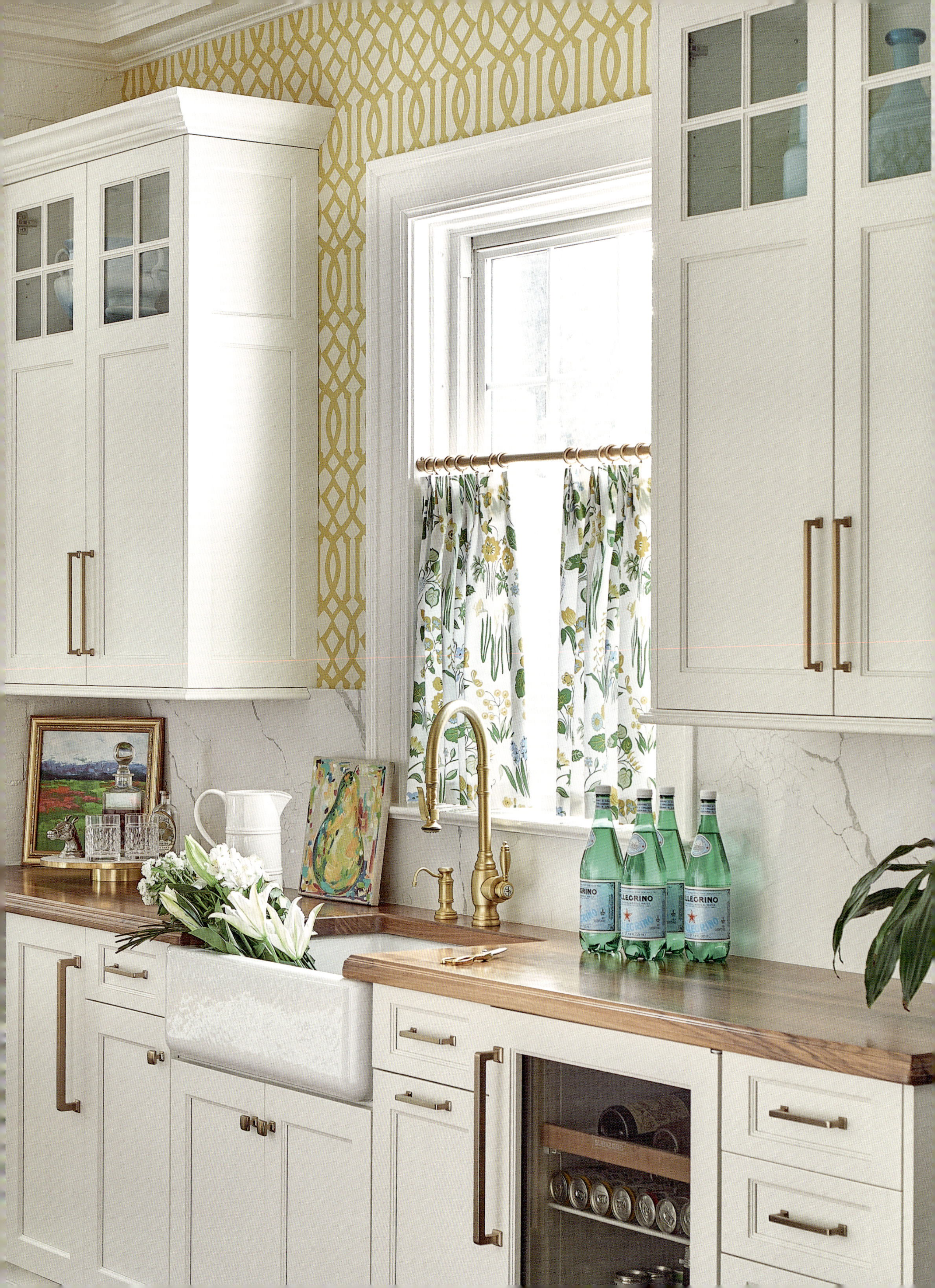

Not every house has a speakeasy! The basement of this more-than-a-century-old home is full of surprises, including a wine cellar and this lounge room that are accessed through the bookcase door.

Schumacher's "Acanthus Stripe" wallpaper is such a grounding focal point in the entry and continues up the staircase onto the landing and to the second story. On the landing, I went with a cheerful magenta and a series of flowers by Tommy Mitchell that represent each member of the family.

While the couple are empty nesters, they wanted each child to have a dedicated bedroom when they visit. The green in this space not only echoes other rooms in the house, but was also inspired by their daughter-in-law's career as a landscape architect.

This palette of this daughter's bedroom plays off the black seen in the nearby green-and-black bedroom. Here, the dark neutral is paired with a punchy magenta for a look that conveys her style.

Pink and green, colors seen in the other children's bedrooms,
fill the youngest daughter's space. The blush tones create a soft,
feminine feel while a blend of modern and traditional elements
also makes it a reflection of her.

A blush bedroom deserves a blush tub. The youngest daughter's adjoining bedroom started the color scheme for this space that was intended to be as playful and girlish as it is sophisticated and chic.

The scale of this branch mural really makes the primary bedroom's design. I wanted it to feel very grand and be the focal point. For balance between masculine and feminine, I paired the navy with light blush accents. It's a nice contrast for a bedroom to feel very strong yet soft at the same time.

We believe that what is now the home's primary bath was originally a sleeping porch. Somewhere down the line, it was turned into a closet before we renovated it to create a spacious bath. Getting creative with mirror placement allowed us to keep the two windows that supply the room's natural light.

# 8

# CHIC STYLE
# for ALL

FAMILY- AND PET-FRIENDLY DESIGNS

Years ago, I attended a decorating weekend with Carleton Varney at The Greenbrier. He asked everyone to close their eyes to envision their childhood bedroom. What patterns did it have? What style? What colors? As we opened our eyes, he said, "I guarantee that is your personal style today." And guess what my childhood home was—chinoiserie! I think it is almost ingrained in us that whatever we grow up being surrounded by still makes us feel comfortable and at home today. That's a big charge when you are designing for families with young children who will not only enjoy the house now but also possibly reflect on it in the future.

The style part comes easily, but with two children of my own and numerous beloved dogs through the years, I know firsthand that homes also have to be practical for everyday living. I'm always thinking about how those two concepts go hand in hand. I absolutely wanted our children, Georgia-Kathryn and Paul, to feel comfortable in our home but I also didn't want it to become a permanent playground for them. I wanted them to learn how to live in and appreciate a beautiful home.

There are several elements and treatments I use in most of my work but especially in spaces where kids and dogs bring life to the home. First, performance fabrics are key. We live in a world where coffee is dribbled, wine is spilt, puppies pounce, and feet need to be propped up. Fabrics that are treated or made for this sort of daily wear and tear make life livable and enjoyable without a lot of fuss. Whether clients think they need this or not, I try to specify these fabrics in places like the family room, breakfast nook, and other gathering spaces.

Applying that same reasoning to flooring, I highly recommend wood floors. Not only are they very forgiving and easy to clean, but they can also create continuity and even give your home a patina. They can be topped off with a natural fiber rug or an inexpensive patterned one to warm them up. If there's an accident, you have the option to clean or even rotate the rug—a solution that doesn't work with wall-to-wall carpet. In entry areas that receive a lot of traffic, indoor/outdoor rugs that can be cleaned with soap and water are especially appreciated.

Last but certainly not least, I make sure to incorporate organization into family homes. My dad ran an orderly household, and it's a trait that I now see in myself. I love for everything to have a place, and I can feel a little crazy when things are scattered. I like to designate drop zones in a home. For example, it might be a place where all the shoes are lined up together, lockers in the garage for sports gear, or cubbies in the mudroom for backpacks. Having these places not only corrals all of life's accessories but also makes the items easy to locate when you need them.

# KIAWAH 25

In a house where there's a little bit of sand and a lot of kids and dogs, it was key to make everything as durable as it is chic. I had worked with this family on their personal home (see Chapter 4), so it was a treat to be able to design their Kiawah Island, South Carolina, getaway as well. Interestingly, I designed this entire project without setting foot on the property until the main pieces of furniture were installed and I went in person to add the next layer of art and accessories. In working with them on their main residence, I had learned how they live as well as their tastes and preferences, making designing the second home a seamless process.

Because it's a destination where the kids will make lifelong memories, we especially wanted it to feel fun and whimsical—a place where the family can really be at home. Built in 1995, the majority of this home's walls were covered in wood paneling. We painted everything in an airy white to give a clean backdrop, and then brought in plenty of color.

As I like to do, I started by introducing the palette in the entry. I wanted this space to be light and fun. It has an air of feeling that you're barefoot, you're going fishing, you're going boating, or you're headed to play golf; in other words, you don't have a care in the world. We commissioned a modern abstract piece by North Carolina artist Kristen Groner that literally had all the colors used inside the home. It hangs front and center as a prelude when you enter.

The adjacent family room picks up on the pinky coral and blue in fabrics, artwork, and even a Slim Aarons photograph that was a perfect fit. A Dorothy Draper fabric for the window treatments became a guiding light for much of the rest of the design. An existing built-in cabinet was completely reworked; the new Chippendale display and

entertainment wall brings a fresh, modern touch to the room. We did keep one element just as we found it—the beautiful stone fireplace. This room flows into the dining area, which was kept casual with a wrapped rattan dining area. We opted not to place a rug under the table, allowing for quick cleanup.

Although not huge, the kitchen is undoubtedly one of the most whimsical rooms in the entire house. The cabinetry is aqua and uses drawers rather than doors to make it easy for little hands to grab snacks or help out with dinner. The wallpaper pattern is sliced lemons, and—along with the bamboo cane pattern on the floor—brings in a cheerful yellow. Those two elements are reminiscent of casual, carefree places, and I was inspired to add the awning that makes it feel like an ice cream stand or pool cabana. The painted wood tile floor is very durable and also hides debris that might be tracked in from a day at the beach or by furry friends. Forgiving quartz countertops, another favorite in family homes, cover the surfaces.

The four-bedroom house has two guest suites upstairs with the primary suite and a third guest suite on the ground floor. The guest suites feature full-on pattern and color, making it a fun, little surprise to open the door and find a playful but still tailored place to escape. The primary bedroom is its own style of retreat, with a more subdued palette to invite rest and a private porch overlooking the sound. The entire home is sophisticated yet casual. If I could have my dream beach house, this would be it.

The family room and dining room are one connected space, thus it was important that the palette, textures, and accent colors carry throughout both. For example, I hung a pair of Julie Neill chandeliers to balance the room overhead. Chinese Chippendale-style bamboo chairs also repeat at the dining table and near the fireplace, while palm fronds add to the island feel.

The family room's cheerful coral palette started with the window treatment fabric, a Dorothy Draper print that features egrets.

I wanted this small kitchen to feel playful but also be really practical. That was my thought in putting all the functional pieces against the side walls and going bold with the aqua on the cabinetry. After covering the ceiling with a whimsical sliced lemon paper, I found a cane-print floor tile that paired perfectly.

Because it's a beach house, a lot of the spaces are bright. But we wanted the primary suite to have a slightly more serene feel with soft blues and natural materials like the wicker chaise and jute rug.

In the primary bath, the view outdoors and the patterned wallpaper both act as art. We kept the rest of the materials classic and neutral, allowing these features to stand out.

Bamboo-inspired furnishings and a wicker picture light pair with
a blue green color that's reminiscent of the marsh view outside
this bedroom.

In the girls' bedroom, I paired a lovely lilac gingham with "Citrus Garden," a well-loved, classic Schumacher fabric that never goes out of style. Each side of the room mirrors the other, creating a perfectly symmetrical scene for the eye.

The fabric on the drapes and pillows was the starting point for the guest suite's design. We loved it so much that we repeated it on the adjoining bath's wallpaper.

Our goal was to make doing laundry like a day at the beach. This whimsical wallpaper and bright-hued cabinetry are both a nod to the tropical setting of the home.

# 9

# BRINGING IT HOME

STEP INTO MY HOUSE

Throughout this book, I've had the joy of sharing a bit of my design philosophy, from how I came to love color to my formula for mixing patterns. I hope you've gotten to know more about what makes my heart sing and the passion that I have for design, as well as finding ideas that will bring joy into your home. But what about my own home? Am I practicing what I preach there? You better believe it!

Every aspect of our home was considered in a sensible fashion in relation to how we truly live. There are big nonnegotiables—like an easily accessible place to store and display all of my heirloom china and silver. And there is the color and pattern I already mentioned that seems to flow naturally into every space I create. You'll also see chinoiserie influences that mimic my own childhood home. These are all mixed with fresh, modern pieces—like an acrylic table here or abstract art there—to keep our home current.

Prior to building this house in 2016, we lived next door for a number of years. We loved the layout of that house and replicated it almost exactly here. The time and experience in that home also allowed us to process the things we would do differently and how certain features (either architectural or decorative) might be adjusted to better serve us in this phase of life. For instance, all of my china and silver were kept in the basement so when I wanted to host a party, I had to schlep the items up piece by piece—not really a practical way to store items you want to see and use all the time. A custom cabinet added in the new home solved that problem. I was also planning to have my studio at our home; I decided to make our dining room a multipurpose space that could easily serve as both a weekday workplace and a weekend gathering space. Other features, including a deeper covered porch and more natural light, especially in the bath, were also considered. My husband, David, has a saying, "You should have sun on your cornflakes and shade on your cocktail." We adhered to that philosophy when positioning our home on the lot, making sure plenty of light poured into just the right spots at just the right time of day.

It probably comes as no surprise that as a designer I've also used our home as a laboratory of sorts—testing out new swatches and treatments. Sometimes I have learned a lesson the hard way, such as the time I painted our bedroom floors white only to have them turn yellow after not receiving enough sun. Luckily, I was able to cover them with black paint for a new look. I've also played with trends here. When our house was built, everyone was just beginning to join the gray movement. I thought, "I work with color all day. Maybe at home I'll do all gray and white and not have any color in our bedroom at all." It drove me nuts! Instead of taking down the scenic investment wallpaper, we literally painted on top of it, a solution that worked here but that I don't suggest for everyone. I'm certain some of you are cringing, but I had to have color back in my life.

While all of these elements—many of which are overarching—were important, it's often the small moments I enjoy the most and that I feel truly make a house a home. Details like the commissioned portraits of our children, the monogrammed cocktail napkins I use with my morning coffee, and the seasonal accents that signal a fresh chapter. These are the extra little Southern graces that set our house apart and make it special to us. I hope you'll enjoy stepping inside to see them for yourself.

# MY PERSONAL HOME

As with all of my projects, I introduced the color palette and overarching details for our house at the front door. Years ago, I saw a door with fretwork similar to ours in a Lilly Pulitzer catalog. I saved it, knowing that if we built again, I would use that as inspiration. Its blue hue carries into our foyer on a wallpaper that was actually my starting point for the entire home. In the last ten to fifteen years, I have been more drawn to blues and really wanted to play that up in this home. I also love that so many other colors pair beautifully with blue. In a few years, I may want to change out the entry's pink accents for a sunny yellow or crisp green, but this blue-and-white paper is here to stay. It's one of my hallmarks.

I continued to develop this palette deeper into the house, using a stronger solid blue in the study to the right of the entry, another rendition of blue-and-white in our family room, and then a cornflower blue in the kitchen. Like many of my clients, David and I love to entertain. The concept for the kitchen, as well as its spacious silver cabinet and pantry, were built around that idea. Working with Ewing Cabinet Company, I crafted a one-of-a-kind piece that is a perfect marriage of Southern style and sensibility. Behind these very stately doors with brass cremone bolts—which are like jewelry in my eyes—lighted drawers roll out to reveal my organized silver pieces. This is a signature feature that really feels like me and definitely makes a statement when you walk into our kitchen. While I have all of these beautiful pieces on display, the bones of our kitchen are concealed in a walk-in pantry. I love to pull items from these spaces, move out the barstools, and place a spread of food on the island for guests to enjoy.

When it is just our family of four, we spend most of our time in the kitchen, the adjacent breakfast room, and family room—it's our hub. My formula of mixing florals,

geometrics, plaids, and solids plays out perfectly here. Art from local artists fills the walls, making it feel personal to us. The same is true in our bedroom. As I said, after living with the gray walls and fabrics for a few years, I absolutely had to reintroduce color in our primary suite. Green differentiates it from the rest of our house but is also a favorite hue that pairs well with the berry- and cantaloupe-colored accents.

In thinking of how to best use the square footage of our home, the dining room was a natural place to serve dual purposes. Dining rooms are often one of the most exquisite spaces in a house yet they seem to get very little use. I reasoned that by creating a custom Chippendale-inspired cabinet to house all of my swatches and work necessities and also by using the dining table as a conference table, I could work in a beautiful, elegant space every day and then simply close the cabinetry and set the table for a party. I kept the walls white to allow my clients' mood boards and presentation pieces to stand out but applied a timeless treillage to them for texture and interest. The table and chairs once belonged to Virginia governor Thomas Stanley and were purchased by my father-in-law at auction and gifted to us. I kept the mahogany finish on the table but painted the chairs white for a more contemporary appeal. One of my favorite things about this space is the retractable doors that open to extend the room's footprint outdoors. It's such a treat to have cocktails outside with friends and then step back indoors to a beautifully set dinner table.

While many elements of my home are timeless and will never change, I love the simple pleasure of adding seasonal accents as the calendar changes or special themed pieces when I'm hosting a gathering. I have summer, fall, and winter salad plates that I rotate to pair with my classic dinner plates. The same with my coffee mugs and cocktail napkins. Every morning, I look forward to grabbing my cup and napkin and seeing what's on top today. I also have an epergne on my entry console whose contents change frequently. It may hold eggs for Easter, ornaments at Christmas, or favors for a shower. I think this gives a first impression of what to expect when you enter the home, especially if you are arriving for a party. It's whimsical, inviting, and puts everyone at ease about the tone of the gathering, which is how I always want guests to feel in our home.

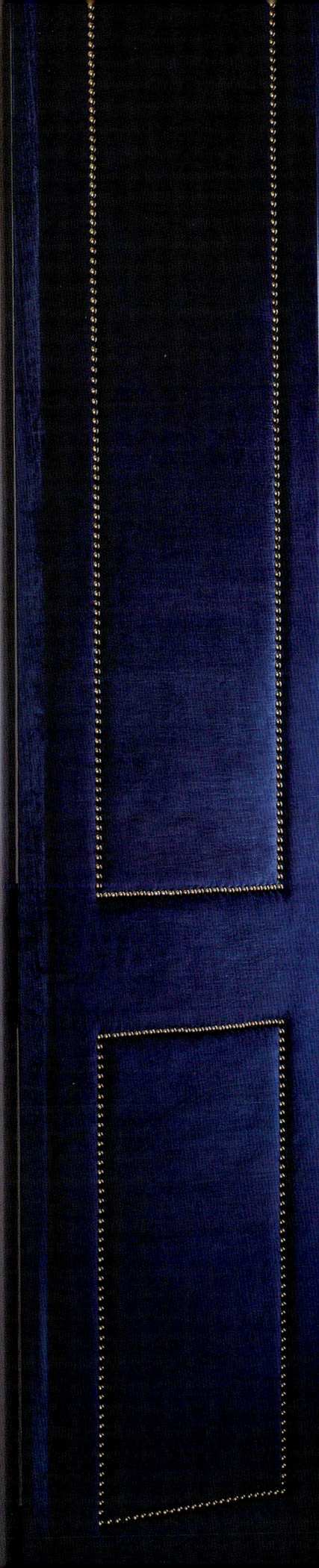

One of my favorite things about our kitchen is the pantry. Hidden behind this paneled door are all of the unsightly but fully necessary things that make a kitchen work. I love that when entertaining, I can keep all of this concealed behind a closed door but also have easy access to it when needed. When we were designing the room, I also added glass-front nooks above the refrigerator and pantry door for display and storage. I put beautiful yet less-frequently used pieces here. It's a feature that is both functional and decorative.

A recent refresh of our family room gave me the opportunity to bring in green alongside the blue that flows into the space from the adjoining breakfast nook. I picked up the artwork over the mantel in an antique shop while traveling, knowing it would be the perfect size and palette for the room.

My husband's family has owned a local Ford dealership for sixty years, which inspired me to use blue in our study. I paired the hue with its complementary color—orange—as an accent and added a marbleized wallpaper to the fifth wall to tie the room together.

Our bedroom is a great example of how I like to mix different scales. The rug's geometric print is oversized, while the drapes are done in a smaller pattern. The side chair is a sentimental piece that belonged to my parents that I reupholstered for use here.

In our son's bedroom, I went with a masculine blue, black, and white palette. The graphic wallpaper on the ceiling is a fun, modern touch for a teenager while the monogrammed shams are a timeless addition that fits with the overall style of our home.

I love using wallpaper as art. In our guest bedroom, I decided to frame two mural panels to layer on top of the lattice print that fills the walls. The thin, gold bamboo frames are a perfect complement to the scheme.

# ACKNOWLEDGMENTS

I would like to extend my deepest gratitude to the incredible people who made this book possible. This project would not have come to life without their support, encouragement, and expertise.

First, to my family, thank you for your endless love, patience, and belief in me. To my husband, David, whose understanding and partnership have been essential in bringing this project to life. Your encouragement in all my design endeavors has meant more than words can express. A special thank you to my two children, Georgia-Kathryn and Paul, whose boundless energy, laughter, and perspective have reminded me of the importance of creativity and balance. Your presence has made this journey even more meaningful. I am forever grateful to my mother, Kathryn, whose unwavering love and support have always been my foundation. Her belief in my vision has been a constant source of inspiration.

I would also like to thank all of my clients who have entrusted me with their spaces. Your vision, trust, and collaboration have been invaluable to the creative process. Each project has been a unique journey, and I am deeply grateful for the opportunity to bring your dreams to life.

To my incredible staff, thank you for your tireless work behind the scenes to bring every project to fruition. This book is as much a reflection of your passion and dedication as it is of my vision. Special thanks to Vicki Gural, Sharon Smith, Lisa Anthony, Hollee Old, and Billie Johnson for everything you've contributed.

A tremendous thank you to my photographers, Susie Peck and Dustin Peck, whose creativity and skill brought this book to life. The images beautifully showcase the designs, and I am forever thankful for your talent.

Thank you to Tiffany Adams, my writer, whose professionalism and dedication guided this book from concept to reality. Your ability to capture my thoughts and design process so beautifully was invaluable.

Lynn Terry, thank you for writing the foreword for *Southern Sensibility*. Your insight and words set the perfect tone for this book, and I am incredibly honored by your contribution. You have been one of my greatest mentors.

To Cheminne Taylor-Smith, your guidance and expertise helped me navigate this process with confidence, and I am grateful for your steady hand throughout.

Thank you to my editors, Juree Sondker and Jennifer Adams, and the entire Gibbs Smith team for your dedication to refining my ideas. Your thoughtful and meticulous work was vital to this project.

Eric Ross, your advice in the early stages of my book journey was invaluable. I appreciate the time and knowledge you shared with me.

Thank you to Tobi Fairley for sharing insights into business practices that have helped shape my firm's success. The coaching from you and your team was one of the best investments I've made.

To my dear friends, thank you for your constant encouragement and belief in me. Your support has been a guiding light, and I am deeply thankful for your wisdom, loyalty, and friendship.

This book reflects the collaboration and support from all of you, and for that, I am truly grateful.

## ABOUT THE AUTHOR

**Creating a sophisticated but casual approach** to today's lifestyles is the focus of Edith-Anne Duncan's interiors and what she does best. Meticulous attention to detail is the trademark that elevates her creations to a higher level.

The expertise and talent that Edith-Anne draws upon come from a multilayered approach to each project. With a strong Southern sensibility, she is inspired by history, travel, fashion, art, color, and technology to incorporate each client's wishes.

With clients from Maryland to Florida, Edith-Anne ensures that each project reflects the unique needs, personality, and lifestyle of the individual client.